The Storm

by Celeste Albright

HOUGHTON MIFFLIN BOSTON

PHOTOGRAPHY CREDITS: Cover © Masterfile Royalty Free; Toc © Kent Wood/Photo Researchers, Inc.; 2 © Andre Jenny/Alamy; 3 © Masterfile Royalty Free; 4 © Workbook Stock/Jupiter Images; 5 © Kent Wood/Photo Researchers, Inc.; 6 © Andrew Fox/Corbis/Corbis; 7 © David R. Frazier Photolibrary, Inc./Alamy, 8 © Jinny Goodman/Alamy; 9 © James Osmond/Alamy; 10 © Donna Day/Getty Images

Printed in India

ISBN-13: 978-0-547-01718-1
ISBN-10: 0-547-01718-9

3 4 5 6 7 8 9 0940 15 14 13 12 11 10

Look at the sky.
A storm is coming.

Look at the clouds.
A big storm is coming.

Look at the trees.
The big storm is here.

Look at the lightning!

Look at the rain come down.

And look at
all the umbrellas!

Oh, look!
The sun is coming out.
The big storm is
going away.

Look at the sun.
And look at
the blue sky.

We can go out and play!

Responding

TARGET SKILL **Sequence of Events** This book is about a big storm. Tell what happens in the beginning, middle, and end of the story.

Write About It

Text to World Draw a picture of a rain storm in the city. Then tell a story about the picture. Remember to tell what happened in the beginning, middle, and end.

WORDS TO KNOW

are	my	with
come	now	you
me	what	

LEARN MORE WORDS

lightning	storm

TARGET SKILL **Sequence of Events**

Tell the order in which things happen.

TARGET STRATEGY **Analyze/Evaluate**

Tell how you feel about the text, and why.

GENRE **Informational text** gives facts about a topic.